C000299536

Little Books of Ireland

Aughanure Castle, Co. Galway

Tullynally Castle, Co. Westmeath

Dunluce Castle, Co. Antrim

Malahide Castle, Co. Dublin

Dunguaire Castle, Co. Clare

Leamaneh Castle, Co. Clare

Blarney Castle, Co. Cork

Glin Castle, Co. Limerick

Clifden Castle, Connemara

Dunboy Castle, Co. Cork

Bunratty Castle, Co. Clare

Lismore Castle, Co. Waterford

Doonagore Tower Castle, Co. Clare

Ross Castle, Killarney

Carrickkildavnet Castle, Co. Mayo

Raheen Castle, Co. Cork

Enniskillen Castle, Co. Fermanagh

Kilkenny Castle, Kilkenny City

Tully Castle, Co. Fermanagh

Rockfleet Castle, Co. Mayo

Johnstown Castle, Co. Wexford

Donegal Castle, Co. Donegal

Kilkea Castle, Co. Kildare

King John's Castle, Limerick City

Minard Castle, Co. Kerry

Ashford Castle, Co. Mayo

Cahir Castle, Co.Tipperary

Park's Castle, Co. Leitrim

BOOKS IN THIS SERIES

Published by Real Ireland Design
Picture House 16/17 Bullford Business Park,
Kilcoole, Co. Wicklow, Ireland.
www.realireland.ie info@realireland.ie

© Picture Press.ie Limited 2002, reprint 2007.

Design Brian Murphy

Photography © Liam Blake

IRISH CASTLES ISBN 0946887209